THINK
BOOKS

the little green book
of BIG green ideas

**Friends of
the Earth**

THINK
BOOKS

A Think Book
First published in Great Britain in 2005 by
Think Books
The Pall Mall Deposit, 124-128 Barlby Road, London W10 6BL
www.think-books.com

Text © Think Publishing 2005
Design and layout © Think Publishing 2005
The moral rights of the author have been asserted

Editor: Sonja Patel
Researched and compiled by: Rhiannon Guy and Matt Packer
Design: Lou Millward, Sub-editor: Sarah Watson
The Little Green team: James Collins, Dinny Gollop, Emma Jones, John Innes,
Mark Searle, Dominic Scott, Helen Smale, Jes Stanfield, Malcolm Tait

Friends of
the Earth

Friends of the Earth
26-28 Underwood Street, London N1 7JQ
www.foe.co.uk

Printed & bound in Great Britain by William Clowes Ltd, Beccles, Suffolk.
The publishers and authors have made every effort to ensure the accuracy and
currency of the information in The Little Green Book of Big Green Ideas.
The publisher and authors disclaim any liability, loss, injury or damage incurred as
a consequence, directly or indirectly, of the use and application of the contents of this
book. As publishing partner, Friends of the Earth welcomes the inclusion but cannot
accept responsibility for the claims of other organisations in this book.

a BIG green thanks

This book has only been made possible with the help and enthusiastic support of many organisations and individuals. They have been credited throughout the pages of this book, and you will also find their contact details at the back should you wish to follow up any little green ideas with some BIG green action.

'One touch of
nature makes
the whole
world kin.'

William Shakespeare

Foreword

Everyone wants – and has a right to – a clean, safe world to live in. Friends of the Earth believes we can all do a bit to bring that about. As consumers, workers, parents, shareholders, voters, volunteers, in the workplace, at home, on our travels – we can all make a difference. The many great ideas in this handy pocket-sized book show how you can help. By taking even small actions in our day to day lives we can all help crack some of the environmental threats facing us today.

The advice comes not only from Friends of the Earth, but a huge variety of organisations and individuals – which just goes to show how widespread the movement for change is. Action for a better world is spreading – from local neighbourhoods to the global stage. People are already making changes and together we can achieve a truly sustainable society – one that looks after the planet and its people at the same time. Read on and find out how you can make a BIG green difference.

Tony Juniper, Executive Director, Friends of the Earth

Want to make a BIG green difference?

Start here...

Turn home appliances off

Home entertainment gadgets like **DVD players use** up to **85%** of the **total** energy they consume while on **standby**

'Want to tackle global issues like climate change? From the moment you wake up, small changes in your day can help the world in big ways.'

Trewin Restorick, Director, Global Action Plan

Save trees

Always try to print on **both sides** of the paper. **Reuse any that's been printed on just** one side **for notes and** shopping lists

'IN EUROPE, THE ENERGY WE USE IN OUR HOMES PRODUCES MORE CLIMATE-CHANGING GREENHOUSE GASES THAN THE WHOLE OF THE TERRITORY'S MANUFACTURING INDUSTRY. EVERY BIT YOU CAN SAVE HELPS.'

ANDREW WARREN, DIRECTOR, ASSOCIATION FOR THE CONSERVATION OF ENERGY (ACE)

Go compost crazy

Paper-based waste like **egg boxes** can be used on the compost heap, as well as all the usual **fruit** and **veg** peelings

'Within a few generations we have turned from HUNTER-GATHERERS into SUPERMARKET BROWSERS. We must rediscover our links with the natural environment if we are to tread more lightly on the world.'

Craig Simmons, Co-founder, Best Foot Forward

Save cash with every cuppa

Only boil the amount of water you **need** for one cup of tea. It will boil quicker and **save** money

'Scientists estimate that the **natural** rate of **extinction** is about four species a year. Yet today, the rate is between **17,000-100,000** each year. It's the biggest mass extinction since the age of **dinosaurs** and almost entirely due to the greed and recklessness of humans.'

Chris Cutter, spokesperson
International Fund for Animal Welfare (IFAW)

Be wise with your money

Carry out a financial **health check:** you could be banking with an *ethical* institution **and** getting an even better deal

'We have to move away from a dumb economy that chews up, spits out and destroys nature and people, towards a smart one that operates with natural cycles: we need to learn to live within our limits.'

Dame Anita Roddick, Activist and Founder of The Body Shop

Make your own lunch

Making your **OWN** lunch instead of buying from a **sandwich shop** saves on packaging, and could also save you **money**

'POOR PEOPLE ARE DIRECTLY DEPENDENT ON BIODIVERSITY AND STRONG ECOSYSTEMS, AND MOST VULNERABLE TO THEIR DEGRADATION. WITHOUT PROPER VALUATION, OUR LOFTY ASPIRATIONS FOR AFRICA WILL NOT BE ACHIEVED.'

Kaveh Zahedi, Acting Director, World Conservation Monitoring Centre (UNEP-WCMC)

Be a
better driver

Drive in the highest gear practicable and avoid using air-conditioning to help **save** on fuel

'In only a hundred years, the global surface temperature has increased by 0.6°C and sea levels have risen by 10-20cm.'

Intergovernmental Panel on Climate Change (IPCC)

Get some plants

Forget air fresheners.

These 'natural air conditioners' can remove up to **87%** of indoor pollution in **24 hours**

'Average annual temperatures across the UK may rise by between 2°C and 3,5°C by 2080.'

DEFRA, Department for the Environment Food and Rural Affairs (UK)

Sow your seeds

Start growing your own tasty **herbs** or **vegetables** in your **garden** or on your kitchen **windowsill.** Save waste **and** money on supermarket goods

'Individuals who care really can make a difference for the better. Believe it and take action.'

Nick Barrett, Chief Executive, The Ramblers' Association

Do it on your doorstep

Use your communal **kerbside** or personal doorstep recycling scheme. Encourage your council to set up **better** recycling facilities

'One way or another, we will learn to live elegantly and frugally within the Earth's natural limits; either with joy in our hearts, or dragged kicking and screaming to the same point. Which way will you choose?'

Jonathon Porritt, Programme Director, Forum for the Future

Tank it up

Save energy with proper tank insulation. A British Standard lagging jacket and pipe **insulation** from tank to boiler can save you **£20 a year**

'Our countryside is a life support mechanism in a predominantly urban world. Just as wildlife depends on it for a home, so do we for calm, recreation and spiritual refreshment.'

Shaun Spiers, Chief Executive,
Campaign for the Protection of
Rural England (CPRE)

Kerb your car

Journeys less than **two miles** may be quicker and involve less **hassle** if you go by foot, bike or bus. Fewer cars means less **pollution**

'I FEEL STRONGLY ABOUT ENVIRONMENTAL ISSUES. BUT I'M NOT A ZEALOT. I DON'T THINK WE SHOULD ALL HAVE TO WEAR HESSIAN UNDERWEAR AND KNIT OUR YOGHURT.'

Ben Elton, comedian and author

Boycott the bags

Billions of plastic carrier bags are handed out in the UK each year. Reuse and **refuse** them where you can

'The most important environmental issue is the lack of conservation ethic in our culture.'

GAYLORD NELSON, FOUNDER OF EARTH DAY

Bring a mug to work

Save **waste** at work.
Use a **mug** or a **glass** for
your **drinks** instead of
disposable cups,
and encourage colleagues
to do the same

'For each of our actions
there are consequences.'
James Lovelock,
environmentalist
and scientist

Coffee grounds

Used coffee grounds make great instant **compost**; they're also great at keeping **slugs** at **bay**

'If deforestation continues at current rates, scientists estimate nearly all tropical rainforest ecosystems will be

destroyed

by the year 2030.'

Rainforest Foundation

'The only thing that can save the world, is the reclaiming of the awareness of the world. That's what poetry does.'

Allen Ginsberg, US poet, 1926-1997

Be battery wise

Batteries don't biodegrade and are difficult to recycle. Use **rechargeable** ones with solar powered rechargers instead

'Water and air, the two essential fluids on which all life depends, have become global garbage cans.'

Jacques Yves Cousteau, explorer and oceanographer, 1910-1997

Off to market

Buy loose **fruit and veg** from a local **market** or **grocer** rather than highly-packaged goods from **supermarkets**. You could save money too

'THE ONLY WAY TO SAVE A RHINOCEROS IS TO SAVE ITS ENVIRONMENT. THERE'S A MUTUAL DEPENDENCY BETWEEN IT AND MILLIONS OF OTHER SPECIES, BOTH ANIMALS AND PLANTS.' Sir David Attenborough, naturalist and TV presenter

Clean green

Use **environmentally friendly cleaning products** and reduce waste by replacing **disposable kitchen roll** with reusable cloths

‘Analyse advertisements carefully.

They are designed to stimulate dissatisfaction.

Don’t believe the hype.’

Low Impact Living

Follow the refill rule

Packets of **washing powders, liquids, salt, herbs** and even bathroom products can be refilled to save on wasteful packaging

'Find out which companies are taking environmental issues seriously. Put the pressure on by writing to those that aren't.'

Ethical Consumer

Join a milkround

Reduce waste

by getting milk **delivered** to your door.

Milk bottles can be

re-used 20 times before

they **have to be recycled**

'The **average** car commuter drives 19 miles a day: car-sharing with one other person can save 640kg of **carbon dioxide** from polluting the atmosphere **every year**.'

LIFTSHARE

Buzz off

Don't waste electricity on plug-in repellents. Use **citronella** candles to keep flies and midges away

'THERE ARE MORE THAN 660,000 EMPTY HOMES IN THE UK. REPORT THEM, OR ANY WASTED PROPERTY, TO YOUR LOCAL AUTHORITY TO STOP NEW ONES BEING BUILT.'

The Empty Houses Association

Police your PC

Remember to switch your office computer and monitor off every time they're not in use – especially at night

'Help your child identify the **10 most common wildflowers, butterflies, trees and garden birds** to kindle an interest and an understanding of the **natural world.**'

Field Studies Council

Borrow, don't buy

Hire videos and DVDs, and **borrow** books from a library or swap with friends to save on **packaging, waste and cash**

'SPEND SMALL BUT DRESS RICH: RECYCLING CLOTHES THROUGH YOUR LOCAL CHARITY STORE CAN SAVE WASTE AND HELP POOR PEOPLE AROUND THE WORLD.'

OXFAM

Pass on your PC

Sell **computers** online, **donate** them to charity or a friend, or find a company which can recycle them

'Since 1930, half the UK's ancient woodlands have been lost by the planting of non-native conifers.'

The Woodland Trust

Be upwardly mobile

Mobiles take **years** to break down. **Recycle** them through a charity or **treat a friend**. Avoid waste altogether by **saying no** to upgrades

'The number of people living in
water-stressed countries is projected
to climb from 470 million to
three billion by 2025.'

Water Aid

Don't just dump

In need of a spring clean?
Sell, recycle or
donate what you don't
want. Have a **clothes
swap** party or join your
local Freecycle group at
www.freecycle.org

'Get stuck into an **environmental project** and get some space **away from it all**. Even pledging a minute a day can help.'

Timebank

Look to the future

Old spectacles can be **donated** to people who desperately need them. Most opticians accept **donations** – ask yours

'Fairtrade has taught us to work in harmony with the environment, avoid polluting clean water supplies and respect natural forests.'

Juan-Luis Rojas, Fairtrade pineapple grower, Costa Rica

Save energy and water

Take a **quick shower** rather than a bath. **Avoid** power showers – they can use as **much** water and energy as a **bath**

'The price of **bananas** in UK supermarkets has fallen 33% in the last two years. Fairtrade provides banana growers with a stable price and a sustainable livelihood.'

Fairtrade Foundation

'Shopping is more American than thinking.'

ANDY WARHOL, US ARTIST, 1928-1987

Perfect pasta

Save energy by boiling pasta for **just** **two minutes.** It will cook by itself if you leave it to stand **in the water** for the full cooking time

'Protect children from junk food. It's messing up their health and destroying the environment.'

SUSTAIN, the alliance for better food and farming

Share your Christmas

Don't throw **unwanted** gifts away. **Give them to charity shops** or pass them on to friends

'Only one quarter of 1% of the world's freshwater is readily useable by people – we can no longer take water for granted.'

Wildfowl and Wetlands Trust

Do you need it?

Ask yourself how much
you really need that
'necessary' item
before you buy it.
The chances are, you,
or someone you know,
already has one

'Stand up for **species:** biodiversity's positive **impact** on local communities can **improve** everything from community **safety** to personal health.'

The Wildlife Trusts

Get a cabbage patch kid

Get **children** into gardening by giving them their own little vegetable patch – and then eat the **fruits** of their labour

'Across Europe, enough mobile phone handsets are discarded each year to make a chain from London to Perth. Recycle.'
Recycool

Join a news feed

Get your daily fix of news and updates online. If you do buy newspapers, recycle them at the end of the week, or shred them for compost

'The plastic used in a typical printer cartridge is expected to take at least 1,000 years to decompose. Over 1 billion of them are discarded every year.'
Recharger magazine

Furnish with care

New furniture can be expensive and is often boring! **Check out** antique fairs and second hand shops for better **quality buys from the past**

'Every person has it within their power to help or harm the environment every day, no matter how old or young they are. Make a choice.'

Peter Littlewood, Director,
Young People's Trust for the Environment
and Nature Conservation (YPTENC)

Be crafty

Making your own cards and presents is a great way to show someone how much you care – and it can save you money too

'Ask your bank how they invest your savings. If they won't tell you, switch to an ethical bank that will.'
Triodos, ethical banking

Recycle Christmas

Wrapping paper can be used again if removed carefully. Plus you can **make new greetings cards** from old

'Work together:
reach out and
connect the vast
missing contribution of
ethnic minority
communities to the
pleasures and
magnificence of the
natural environment.'
Black Environment
Network

One hob meals

Pressure cookers and stackable steamers let you cook several different foods on **one** hob

'Nearly three billion nappies are thrown away in the UK each year. The vast majority of them – 90% in fact – end up as landfill.'

Real Nappy Campaign

Ten to a tool

Share your tools with friends or neighbours. Does everyone in the street need a **lawnmower**, a workbench or a **steam cleaner**?

'Buying organic food from a box scheme or farmers' market helps supports wildlife, the local economy, reduces transport and pollution, and saves you money.'

The Soil Association

Citrus fresh

Get chopping boards and work surfaces extra clean with the juice of a lemon to avoid using chemical cleaning products. Simply rub and rinse off

'When is a holiday not a holiday? When it's a Guilt Trip, exploiting workers, destroying the environment and contributing to global injustice.'

Tourism Concern

Put a lid on it

Cover your saucepans and save energy and money with every meal

'The average person in the UK
uses 150 litres of water a day.
In the US, it's 600 litres a day.
In Sub-Saharan Africa
it's 10 litres a day.'

**World Development
Movement (WDM)**

Spice moths out

Mothballs can be **chemical**. Sprinkle cupboards with **cedarwood oil** to flush moths out. Bags of **lavender** will keep them away **too**

'The average person makes **400** car trips a year; **58%** of them are less than **five** miles and could be made by **bike**.'

SUSTRANS, routes for people

Be a stain angel

Carpet stain removers contain toxic substances that are harmful to you and the environment. Try soda water or sparkling water instead

'Flying has a huge impact on the environment. If you can't avoid it, make sure you offset your carbon emissions by planting a tree. '

Environmental Change Institute

Nice ice

Opt for an **energy-efficient** fridge or freezer when you buy. **Ask the retailer** if they can take your **old** appliance for reconditioning

'In some parts of
the world, the bodies
of whales
and dolphins washed
ashore are so
highly contaminated they
qualify as toxic waste.'

Whale and Dolphin
Conservation Society (WDCS)

Time your temperature

One of the easiest ways to **save energy and money** is to put your heating on a timer. In summer, just turn it off

'If it's the last thing you do, get a tree instead of a headstone.'

Natural Death Movement

Buy in bulk

Keep the cost and waste of everyday items down, by picking up items in bulk. You could even share orders with a friend

'300 million gallons of raw or partially treated sewage are discharged around the UK coastline each day. Campaign to keep your beaches clean.'

Surfers Against Sewage (SAS)

Throw open the windows

Don't spritz smells with chemicals. Opening windows lets **musty smells out** and fresh air in

'We have to move
from Three Planet Living
to One Planet Living.
The way we live now is
like taking money from
the bank and putting
none back in.'

Andrew Lee,
Director of Campaigns,
World Wildlife Fund
(WWF)

Pedal power

Pick up **second hand** bikes, at a snip of the price of new bikes, from reputable stores or online. Save money on **air-polluting transport** and get some **exercise**

'When you buy a garment, ask where and under what conditions it was made. Insist on a response.'

No Sweat

Let it rain

Rainwater is good for your outdoor plants and can be collected for indoor ones too. Just stick them outside in time for the next rain shower

'Carbon dioxide from burning fossil fuels – oil petrol and natural gas – makes up 80% of carbon emissions from industrialised countries.'

The Carbon Trust

Take it from the tap

EU laws ensure UK water is safe to drink.

Bottled water wastes plastic, it's expensive, and is often transported from abroad

'Every year, an estimated 17.5 billion plastic bags are given away by supermarkets: that's 290 bags for every person in the UK.'

Wastewatch

Wrap wisely

Aluminium foil can be used more than once or recycled. **Greaseproof paper** can be composted. Or you can cover leftover food with a plate

'My hope is that the natural world is more resilient than we give it credit for, and that we still have enough time to act.'

Zac Goldsmith,
Editor, The Ecologist

Cut your cycle

Even new 'eco-friendly' **washing machines** use 50 litres of water per wash. Try and wear clothes more than once. Some may just need airing outside

'The UK produces enough rubbish each year to fill 3.5 million double decker buses: enough to stretch from London to Sydney and back.'

Recycle Now

Keep
kettles clear

Remove limescale from your **kettle** with **vinegar** **and water. Then boil with** fresh water. Water plants with the remains, **once cooled**

'Experts believe there are now between 5,000 and 7,000 tigers left in the wild – far less than the number currently held in private hands in the US.'

Convention on International Trade in Endangered Species (CITES)

Bless you

Use a **cotton handkerchief** to blow your nose instead of packs of tissues.

This saves on packaging and **trees**

'Approximately 12 billion litres of paint are sold world-wide every year. About two billion litres are stored, hoarded, unused or disposed of.'

Community Repaint

Be better bread

Stale bread can be used for **breadcrumbs, bread and butter pudding, bread sauce,** or as **croutons** for soup. The **birds will appreciate** your leftover crusts too

'About two million PCs end up in landfill or storage every year in the UK. In the developing world, 99% of school children never see one at all.'

Computeraid International

Scrub up your act

You can make your own **pan scourers** using the nets that oranges come in. This saves on waste and saves money

'Reduce food miles: buying local produce can reduce associated carbon emissions by almost 100%.'

National Farmers' Retail and Markets Association (FARMA)

Use your oats

Instead of buying expensive and harsh bath foams, infuse your bath with oats. Tie them in a muslin pouch – they'll leave skin soft and silky

'If your **tap drips** once a second, you are wasting **1,500 litres** of water a year.'

Green Futures magazine

Better booze

Organic beer and wine is easy to buy online or pick up from farmers' markets. If you live near a brewery, you can often buy direct, meaning you'll cut down on transport too

'By 2050, travel and tourism will be responsible for 15% of the world's carbon emissions. Make your trip environmentally friendly.'

Green Globe 21

Paint it green

Choose natural paints with the lowest VOC (volatile organic compounds) rating to keep chemicals out of your newly decorated home

'The first UK print run of JK Rowling's Harry Potter and the Half-Blood Prince stretched to two billion pages – that's the equivalent of 8,333 trees.

Read but recycle.'

Barry Crow, Founder,
Green Metropolis

Save with every flush

Save **three litres of water** with every flush. **Put a** plastic bottle filled with water **in your cistern** or see **www.hippo-the-watersaver.co.uk**

'If you want to change the world you must begin from where you are.'

Roger Budgeon, Founder,
The Green Shop

Send it again

Recycle old envelopes by simply using them again. Just **cross out the address** or cover with a label

'Babies are now being born with toxic chemicals from everyday household products contaminating their bodies. Cut these chemicals out.'

Greenpeace

Pest patrol

Avoid pesticides by attracting creatures that naturally prey on your garden pests – a few logs will attract slug-loving hedgehogs and frogs

'Diamonds can fund earth-destroying conflict and human rights abuse. Ask for a certificate confirming country of origin and how they were sold.'

Global Witness

Stop lofty leaks

Insulating your loft can make your home **energy efficient**, saving both fuel and substantial annual costs

'A staggering seven out of every 10 butterfly species are declining in the UK, largely due to human activity. These losses can be reversed by careful action. Their future really is within our hands.'

Dr Martin Warren,
Chief Executive,
Butterfly Conservation

Dust it

Dust the coils at the back of the fridge. Dusty coils can waste up to **30% extra** electricity than clean ones

'The Amazon rainforest produces around 50% of the world's oxygen. Go and plant trees in Ecuador or recycle paper to help save it where you can.'

i-TO-i,
volunteering abroad

Be sewage savvy

**Do you really need to
flush every time?
If it's yellow,
let it mellow.
If it's brown,
flush it down.**

'Remember to use the three Rs and in order:

Reuse, Reduce, Recycle.'

Oneworld

'Nature is able to improve the quality of our lives and everyone is entitled to experience it; visit your local nature areas and get involved in looking after them.'
English Nature

Work it!

If your company doesn't have a **recycling scheme**, don't sit back and wait for someone else to sort it out. **Do it yourself**

'The threats to coral reefs and their ecosystems place the sustainable development of communities, global biodiversity and the health of the oceans in serious jeopardy.'

International Coral Reef Initiative (ICRI)

BBQ friendly

Buy **locally produced charcoal** for your barbie, to help stop tropical rainforests being **chopped down** for charcoal

'Up to 40% of household waste can be composted at home, saving 20% of the UK's methane emissions from the slow decomposition of biodegradable landfill waste.'

The Composting Association

'Everyone uses nature's gifts: they are the source of our food and fuel, clothing and shelter, clean water and air. Their sustainable management needs to be considered in all our decisions.'

World Conservation Monitoring Centre (UNEP-WCMC)

Good wood guide

Ask your retailer where the wood came from for your furniture or decorative items. It could be sourced from diminishing forests

'We shall require a substantially new manner of **thinking** if mankind is to survive.'

Albert Einstein
scientist
1879-1955

Green your teeth

Leaving the tap running while you brush your teeth wastes water. Use a glass or short bursts from the tap

'It's a morbid observation, but if everyone on earth just stopped breathing for an hour, the greenhouse effect would no longer be a problem.'

Jerry Adler, US actor

Cash for cans

Recycling aluminium and steel cans **saves energy and resources.** Some schemes even pay you for recycling them

'When one tugs at a single thing in nature, one finds it attached to the rest of the world.'

John Muir, Scottish naturalist and conservationist, 1838-1914

Let your lawn grow

Help your lawn to conserve water by letting it grow longer. This also encourages wildflower species and lets grass re-seed itself

'There is more stupidity than hydrogen in the universe, and it has a longer shelf life.'

Frank Zappa,
US musician, 1940-1993

Make toast

Use a toaster rather than a grill to **bronze your bread**. It uses less electricity and is less likely to burn

'The most political act we do on a daily basis is eat.' Professor Jules Pretty, sustainable agriculture guru

Cooking good

Chop vegetables up smaller to save on cooking time. Boil water in the kettle first, and use a hob that fits your pan or you'll be heating air

'Peace is the most important pre-condition for sustainability... Poverty is one of the most toxic elements in the world.'

Klaus Topfer, Chief Executive, United Nations Environment Programme (UNEP)

Holiday at home

Aviation emissions contribute to climate change, so explore your own country before you jet off. There are some amazing places to explore right on your doorstep

'The sun is the most readily available source of heat there is – and the cheapest. Make the most of it.'

National Energy Foundation

Don't join the traffic jam

Use the train for longer journeys rather than the car. If you plan ahead, commuting time, fuel and pollution can all be cut this way. Advance fares can also be cheaper

'If we can build long-term thinking into our short-term actions, we'll be part way towards understanding our effect on this planet.'

Malcolm Tait,
Nature writer

Go for greener salad

Bagged salad can contain chemicals and may have **travelled miles** to arrive at your plate. Avoid bagged stuff or **grow your own**

'**Destroying**
rainforest for
economic gain
is like burning
a **Renaissance**
painting to cook
a meal.'
**Edward O Wilson,
US biodiversity expert**

Save water

Help plants conserve water by mulching with **pebbles, bark** or **cut grass.** You can **recycle broken crockery** this way too

'Nature has ceased to be what it always had been – what people needed protection from. Now nature tamed, endangered, mortal – needs to be protected from people.'
Susan Sontag, US author, 1933-2004

What's your footprint?

Flying is the fastest growing contributor to **climate change**.

Plant trees to offset your carbon '**footprint**', or find a way to travel overland

'Dream the world you want and deserve to live in. Write it down. Communicate your vision passionately, as if your life depended upon it!' Randy Hayes, Founder, Rainforest Action Network (RAN)

Bite-sized baddies

Mini packs of food mean more **packaging**. If you need a snack, try a locally grown apple instead

'The 1990s are estimated to have been the warmest decade in the Northern Hemisphere in the past 1,000 years.'

Met Office (UK)

'As a society, we must adapt to climate change: we need to cut waste, reduce energy and protect water as a valuable resource.'

The Environment Agency (UK)

Boycott the biro

Invest in a refillable pen
to **save on plastic**.
Not only will your
writing look better,
**your pen is less likely
to go 'walking' too**

'To forget how to dig the earth and tend the soil is to forget ourselves.'
Mohandas K Gandhi,
Indian freedom fighter,
1869-1948

Think before you print

Technology isn't saving as much **paper** as it should be. **Add a note to the bottom of your emails asking recipients to file, not print**

'There's so much pollution in the air now, that if it weren't for our lungs there'd be no place to put it all.' Robert Orben, US comedian

Police your WC

Don't throw **cotton buds, nappies, condoms** or **sanitary** products down the toilet – they end up on **beaches** and in **lakes** and in **rivers**

'Walking is the safest, most healthy and greenest form of transport. At least 30 minutes a day will add to your life expectancy without burning an ounce of carbon.'

THE RAMBLERS' ASSOCIATION

Wear plants not plastic

The process of making **polyester** generates CO_2, while **cotton** absorbs it as it grows

‘WE DO NOT INHERIT THE EARTH FROM OUR ANCESTORS, WE BORROW IT FROM OUR CHILDREN.’

Native American proverb

'By taking even small actions in our day to day lives, we can help crack some of the environmental threats facing us today.'

Tony Juniper,
Executive Director,
Friends of the Earth

Friends of the Earth inspires solutions to environmental problems, which make life better for people

Friends of the Earth

Friends of the Earth is:

● the UK's most influential national environmental campaigning organisation

● the most extensive environmental network in the world, with around one million supporters across five continents, and more than 70 national organisations worldwide

● a unique network of campaigning local groups, working in more than 200 communities throughout England, Wales and Northern Ireland

● dependent on individuals for over 90% of its income.

To join Friends of the Earth, please call us on 020 7490 1555 between 9am-5.30pm or visit www.foe.co.uk. To find out more about Friends of the Earth's work, or to find your nearest Friends of the Earth local group, call our Information Service on Freephone 0808 800 1111 between 9am-5.30pm. All the tips provided by Friends of the Earth, located on the left-hand pages of this book, can be found at www.foe.co.uk/living.

**Get in touch.
Take action.**

Contacts

ACE
www.ukace.org
020 7359 8000

Anita Roddick Communications
www.anitaroddick.com
www.TakeItPersonally.org

Best Foot Forward
www.bestfootforward.com
01865 250818

Black Environment Network
www.ben-network.org.uk
01286 870715

BTCV (Green Gym)
www.btcv.org
01302 572244

Butterfly Conservation
www.butterfly-conservation.org
0870 774 4309

The Carbon Trust
www.thecarbontrust.co.uk/energy
0800 085 2005

CITES
www.cites.org
+41 22 917 8140

Community Repaint
www.communityrepaint.org.uk
0113 243 8777

The Composting Association
www.compost.org.uk
0870 160 3270

Computeraid International
www.computeraid.org
020 7281 0091

CPRE
www.cpre.org.uk
020 7981 2800

DEFRA (UK)
www.defra.gov.uk
0845 933 5577

Earth Day
www.earthsite.org (March 20)
www.earthday.net (April 22)

The Ecologist magazine
www.theecologist.org
020 7351 3578

The Empty Houses Association
www.emptyhomes.com
020 7828 6288

English Nature
www.english-nature.org.uk
01733 455000

The Environment Agency (UK)
www.environment-agency.gov.uk
0870 8506 506

Environmental Change Institute
www.eci.ox.ac.uk
01865 275848

Ethical Consumer
www.ethicalconsumer.org
0161 226 2929

Fairtrade Foundation
www.fairtrade.org.uk
020 7405 5942

FARMA
www.farma.org.uk
0845 458 8420

Field Studies Council
www.field-studies-council.org
01743 852100

Forum for the Future
www.forumforthefuture.org.uk
020 7324 3630

Friends of the Earth
www.foe.co.uk
0808 800 1111

Global Action Plan
www.globalactionplan.org.uk
020 7405 5633

Global Witness
www.globalwitness.org
020 7272 6731

Green Futures magazine
www.greenfutures.org.uk
020 7324 3660

Green Globe 21
www.greenglobe21.com
+61 (0)26 257 9102

Green Metropolis
www.greenmetropolis.com
contact by email online

Greenpeace
www.greenpeace.org.uk
020 7865 8100

The Green Shop
www.greenshop.co.uk
01452 770629

ICRI
www.icriforum.org
contact by email online

IFAW
www.ifaw.org
020 7587 6700

IPCC
www.ipcc.ch
+41 (0)22 730 8254

i-TO-i
www.i-to-i.com
0870 333 2332

Liftshare
www.liftshare.co.uk
0870 078 0225

Low Impact Living
www.lowimpact.org
01296 714184

Met Office (UK)
www.met-office.gov.uk
0870 900 0100

National Energy Foundation
www.natenergy.org.uk
01908 665555

Natural Death Movement
www.naturaldeath.org
0871 288 2098

No Sweat
www.nosweat.org.uk
07904 431959

Oneworld
www.oneworld.net
020 7239 1400

Oxfam
www.oxfam.org
0870 333 2700

Rainforest Foundation
www.rainforestfoundationuk.org
020 7251 6345

The Ramblers' Association
www.ramblers.org.uk
020 7339 8500

RAN
www.ran.org
+1 (0)41 5398 4404

Real Nappy Campaign
www.realnappycompaign.com
0845 850 0606

Recharger magazine
www.rechargermag.com
+1 (0)70 2438 5557

Recycle Now
www.recyclenow.com
0845 331 3131

Recycool
www.recycool.org
www.wrap.org.uk

SAS
www.sas.org.uk
01872 553001

The Soil Association
www.soilassociation.org
0117 314 5000

Sustain
www.sustainweb.org
020 7837 1228

SUSTRANS
www.sustrans.org.uk
0117 926 8893

Timebank
www.timebank.org.uk
0845 456 1668

Tourism Concern
www.tourismconcern.org.uk
020 7133 3330

Triodos
www.triodos.co.uk
0117 973 9339

UNEP
www.unep.org
+25 (0)42 062 1234

Wastewatch
www.wastewatch.org.uk
020 7549 0300

Water Aid
www.wateraid.org
020 7793 4500

WCMC
www.unep-wcmc.org
01223 277314

WDCS
www.wdcs.org
0870 870 0027

WDM
www.wdm.org.uk
020 7737 6215

Wildfowl and Wetlands Trust
www.wwt.org.uk
0870 334 4000

The Wildlife Trusts
www.wildlifetrusts.org
0870 036 7711

The Woodland Trust
www.woodland-trust.org.uk
01476 581135

WWF
www.wwf.org.uk
01483 426444

YPTENC
www.yptenc.org.uk
01483 539600

more BIG green ideas from Think Books

**Go M.A.D! Go Make a Difference: 2
Over 500 daily ways to save the planet!**

ISBN 0-95413-632-2

**Super Kids: Over 200 incredible ways
for kids to save the planet**

ISBN 1-84525-001-X

THINK
BOOKS

www.think-books.com